HMRD Cesidio Tallini

# Ryamecah Declaration of Indigenous Independence

# Ryamecah Declaration of Indigenous Independence

ISBN-10: 1482510553
ISBN-13/EAN-13: 978-1482510553

# Dedication

This book is dedicated to dead,
non-white, non-European men,
and to their families, bands or
tribes; the forgotten, or never
acknowledged ancestors of
some of those who live in
Winnecomac today; but the
ancestors also to those who,
like the author of this book,
wish to restore their spirit, and
all that was good about them.
May their souls live again on
this good land, and may true
justice and decency prevail.

# Index

# Preface

In school, most Americans are taught the convenient myth that the American Revolutionary War (1775–1783) was a 'revolution'. In reality, that conflict was both a civil war and a revolution.

The American Revolution as a civil war meant divided loyalties. The conflict was not merely the unanimous uprising of Americans against a distant British Empire, but something more divisive and complex.

There were Americans who wanted to preserve their British citizenship, and there were others who wanted a separate political order distinct from that of Mother Britannia. The situation was even more complex than that, as complex as the multiple motives and wishes of all Americans.

To George Washington, Americans loyal to Great Britain were "Unhappy wretches! Deluded mortals." On the opposite side, British General James Robertson had a similar view. He wrote: "I never had an idea of subduing the Americans. I meant to assist the good Americans to subdue the bad."

It wasn't 'them' verses 'us', as Americans are lead to believe in their short, jingoistic, historical synopses passing for an historical education in American high schools. In reality, Americans themselves were deeply divided into Patriot and Loyalist camps, and the former were often called *Americans*, *Whigs*, *Revolutionaries*, *Congress-Men* or *Rebels* by the Loyalists, and the latter were often called *Tories*, *Royalists*, or *King's Men* by the Patriots.

Although over the eight years of the American Revolutionary War people probably changed camps, and perhaps they changed camps even more than once, most estimates place one-third of Americans as Loyalists, one-third on the fence, to be swayed by whomever was winning at the moment, and one-third as Patriots.

Americans know that the Patriots fought for independence from Great Britain, and they are mostly the people that they hear about in school. They don't normally hear about the Loyalist side of the war, nor do they hear about their fate during and after the conflict. In some areas, the civil war was less apparent because one side predominated. In much of Virginia, Pennsylvania, and New England, rebellious Americans successfully suppressed Loyalism, just as the British effectively squelched any pockets of sympathy for the Patriots in Canada. More often than not, however, both sides often waged a bloody civil conflict in many other places such as on the coastline, in the Lower South, in New Jersey, New York, and the lands west of the Appalachian Mountains. Loyalists often faced ostracism, confinement, civil disabilities, and, on rare occasion, death. The only easy way to avoid detection and punishment was to take the loyalty oath often required by Patriots.

The conflict can even be broken down by political ideology and/or religious belief. Patriots could generally be found among Congregationalists, Presbyterians, Low Church Anglicans (who sought a Church of England independent of the State apparatus), those who sought to foster America's economic independence, and those who supported westward expansion. Loyalists could generally be found among High Church Anglicans (who sought greater fusion of Church and State), employees of the Crown, those who sought to limit American expansion, civilians who depended upon British military protection, and those who supported British mercantile policy.

To complete the picture, there were also those who did not wish to fight during the revolution who were Quakers, and they were often mistakenly referred to as Loyalists. There were also Neutralists, those who either didn't want to fight, lived too far away from the areas of conflict, or believed in both Loyalist and Patriot principles. Then there were also German hired soldiers called Hessians, and these were paid by the British government or Parliament to fight on the British side.

The British Province of New York started its existence in 1664, when the Dutch colony of New Amsterdam was taken over by the English and renamed New York. The Dutch did attempt to recover New York in 1673, but the eastern towns refused to submit to the Dutch governor. By the Treaty of Westminster in 1674, Long Island became a part of the British colony of New York. The British

2

Province of New York was organised in 1683, and Long Island at the time contained three of the original twelve counties: Kings, Queens, and Suffolk. Back then, Queens County included all of today's Nassau County, as well as a small portion of western Suffolk County.

From the later part of the 17th century, to the early part of the 18th century, Long Island colonists became self-sufficient in many ways. They enjoyed the freedom of running their day-to-day lives without much interference from British authorities. Great Britain did send governors to some of the colonies to help set up the rules and run the government, but otherwise practised a 'live and let live' philosophy.

Around 1760 the situation began to change. The British had 10,000 troops in North America at the end of the French and Indian War (1754–1763), and they felt they were spending a great deal of money to defend the colonies. By the war's end, the British also found themselves in debt to the tune of 140 million pounds, an enormous sum for those times. So Great Britain began to desire greater control over the colonies, and wanted to tax them in order to pay for the British Empire's huge bills.

The taxes didn't go down well, particularly the one on whale oil, which is not even mentioned in most high school history books. Whaling, a much maligned occupation today for environmental reasons, was a big industry on Long Island back then, and a whaling tax could hurt many people. Other taxes were placed on goods such as glass, lead, paint and paper, and the Stamp Act of 1765 put a tax on all legal documents.

To add insult to injury, there was also greater enforcement of the taxes than ever before, there was a sugar tax, a tax on imported items such as silks, wines and potash, and the most unpopular tax of them all, the tea tax.

Moreover, new rules were issued. Long Islanders resented the new rules that said they could only trade with Great Britain. But the act that probably inflamed the colonists the most back then was the Quartering Act, which forced American colonists to house and feed British forces who were serving in North America.

On 17 March 1776, the British fleet retreated to Halifax, Nova Scotia to refit after the end of the year-long Siege of Boston. Washington, who had successfully taken Boston, expected a new attack on New York. He moved his troops to Long Island and New York City, arriving there himself on 13 April, and reinforced fortifications.

On 2 July 1776, Major General William Howe landed on Staten Island without opposition with 9,300 men. After receiving reinforcements from his brother, Admiral Richard Howe, as well as other Hessian and British reinforcements from England, and also the men in the expedition that had failed to capture Charleston, Howe had over 31,000 troops. When he began operations in August, 24,400 of these men were fit for duty. On 27 August 1776, General Howe soundly defeated General George Washington's forces at the Battle of Long Island in a brilliant tactical display. However, instead of pursuing the Americans and making their defeat complete, he halted. This allowed the Americans to pull off their own brilliant operation in evacuating from the area between 29 and 30 August.

While most of the battle was concentrated in western Long Island, British troops were also deployed to the east to capture the entire 120 mile (193 kilometres) length of Long Island to Montauk. The British met little or no opposition in this operation. Perhaps they were not as unpopular as we are often lead to believe by jingoistic history books, or perhaps Long Island colonists were behaving as peacefully as the Native American tribes that preceded them, and a few peaceful Native Americans still lived on the island as well.

Nassau County was originally the eastern 70 percent of Queens County when New York was divided into twelve counties in 1683. The county originally contained two towns: the Town of Hempstead and the Town of Oyster Bay. During the American Revolutionary War, the Town of Hempstead was split into two when Patriots in the north formed the new Town of North Hempstead, leaving Loyalist majorities in the Town of Hempstead. Long Island as a whole, however, remained a British stronghold until the end of the war.

Despite all the unpopular taxes, most of them later repealed except for the tea tax; despite the real indignities probably suffered by the colonists because of the Quartering Act; Long Island largely remained Loyalist, and the British left New York City only in 1783, or at the end of the American Revolutionary War, when they evacuated the city as agreed in the Treaty of Paris (1783). Not only Long Island had a majority with Loyalist sympathies, but after the British forced General Washington off Manhattan, the area of New York City and Long Island actually became a magnet for displaced Loyalists. Many historians in fact cite this as an example of New York's ambivalence, if not outright opposition to the Revolution.

What was the treatment of Long Island Loyalists at the end of the war, or even of those who had been neutral? Well, they were just as much Americans as the Patriots were, even though the Patriots had monopolised the word 'American' just as some politicians today unfairly appropriate the word 'conservative', and then tax as recklessly as the worst Liberal, but that is not how they were treated by their fellow Americans.

When the British lost, there was nothing for most Loyalists to do but leave the country, and face an uncertain future. The numbers that left were also extraordinary, since it actually became the largest exodus in American history.

At least 60,000 Loyalists left the colonies during and immediately following the war — estimates put the figure as high as 100,000 though — and of these at least 35,000 were New York State residents, including Long Islanders. Many went to the British Isles, and some to the British West Indies. Most however, went to what would later become Canada, where British officials promised free land. This land included Nova Scotia, the fourteenth colony of British North America which never joined the union. At the time of the mass exodus, the area of the Saint John River was part of Nova Scotia, but a Loyalist influx of about 14,000 led Great Britain to create a new province, New Brunswick.

These American men and women braved frigid winters, sickness and loneliness, and tried to carve out a new life from the bleak wilderness. Few came back, and a few became prominent. Edmund Fanning, who was born in Riverhead, Long Island, and commanded a regiment of Loyalist troops, later became lieutenant governor of Nova Scotia.

But historians generally don't mention just how many of the large estates of the Loyalists were later confiscated by the newly minted and arrogant states, New York State among these. Today that behaviour would be called 'un-American', but that was actually the typical behaviour of those who, having won the war, but who never even tried to secure the peace, treated Loyalists with scorn and contempt, and even worse.

What is also not conveniently mentioned by historians is that the confiscations of the properties of the Loyalists were Treaty of Paris violations by the newly-recognised thirteen sovereign states. In the ten articles of the Treaty of Paris it was agreed by both Great Britain and the United States in Article 5 that the Congress of the Confederation would earnestly recommend state legislatures to recognise the rightful owners of all confiscated lands, and to provide for the restitution of all estates, rights, and properties belonging to the Loyalists that had been confiscated. Article 6, on the other hand, obligated the United States to prevent future confiscations of the properties of Loyalists. However, while the Treaty of Paris specified the *status quo ante bellum*, the 'state existing before the war' principle in the treatment of private properties, the United States chose to ignore the two conditions of the Treaty of Paris and to impose *uti possidetis* at the war's end, the 'as you possess' principle. This firmly established, right from the beginning, the United States' future reputation as a treaty breaker — from the Treaty of Fort Pitt in 1778, to the Treaty of New Echota of 1835, the history of the United States, even versus Native American tribes, has been nothing but a trail of broken treaties.

Today, after a trail of abuses that practically goes all the way to the Moon, where they should have planted the Long Island flag, not the United States flag, the same political entity even violates the spirit of the Tenth Amendment of its own constitution, part of the highest law of the land, and the only law which protects the sovereignty of US states despite the Law of Nations preventing it.

The founders of the United States went to great lengths to balance institutions of the US government against each other (eg, balancing power among the three branches: Congress, the President, and the Supreme Court; between the House of Representatives and the Senate; between the federal government and the states; and among states of different sizes, and regions with different interests). However, they accomplished this with less than satisfactory results under a human rights perspective. There are agencies of the US government which largely act as true public servants, such as the United States Postal Service (USPS), but which are so overburdened by federal (Congress) and Internal Revenue Service (IRS) regulation that now they either provide full-time employment with full benefits such as annual leave, sick leave, and health insurance, but only to the old work force, or they provide even the most desirable and productive new worker only with casual employment (aka contingent, temporary or precarious work in other countries), which in the United States means you can work only less than 1,000 hours per 12-month calendar year. There are also agencies of the US government which largely do not act as true public servants, such as the Food and Drug Administration (FDA), which are so underburdened by regulation that they in fact serve as agents for the actual destruction of human rights, all in favour of corporate and/or professional rights.

If the founders of the United States went to great lengths to balance institutions of the US government against each other, and with less than satisfactory results, however, since there is no permanent body of government with great power, and specifically designed to limit the power of the federal, state, local and other government agencies to encroach on the rights of citizens, the founders really left a government ill-suited for the long term protection and preservation of human rights. You have very productive and socially redeeming workers who can only find either minimum wage employment, casual employment, or no employment at all past the age of 50, and then you have socially non-redeeming workers in Congress with full-time employment, full benefits, additional perks nobody else has, with work well past the age of 80, and to whom their very own legislation does not even have to personally apply!

It is a fact: British Loyalists united the land of the whole of Long Island even during the American Revolution. It is they who deserve our esteem today, despite their all too human flaws, and perhaps it is they, and fellow Commonwealth citizens around the world, some whose ancestors even came from Long Island, who can show us the way to the most decent and prosperous future. Despite its strong ethnic and religious diversity, British Loyalists made Long Island an English-speaking island, and a haven of peace and civility while the continent was in chaos. Even the uppity Manhattan (the Manhattan island tribe) benefited from their presence while it lasted. Shame on them for their terrible sachem, who makes himself big on all the *wampum* (gold or printed money) he has!

After the war, so-called American Patriots, who are really mongrels of the Mahican and the Mohawk (the criminal tribes who slaughtered our peaceful Winnecomac tribes), divided and conquered our land, and they in fact started this conquest with the illegally confiscated property of Long Island Loyalists!

Later, in their unstoppable westward expansion, they almost drove Native Americans towards extinction, as well as the buffalo and the bald eagle.

Later still, the Manhattan (the Manhattan island tribe) showed themselves to be a non-Winnecomac, non-Long Island tribe, and following the 1898 formation of the City of Greater New York, they have separated the Canarsie from the Merrick (Mericoke), the Rockaway from the Massapequa (Marsapeague), bringing us backwards instead of forwards, back to a time when two of these tribes spoke Dutch, and two spoke English.

Finally, the Mohawk (the United States tribe who still treats Long Island tribes like a colony and a cash cow) have never truly stopped their reckless westward expansion, and after even bombing Hiroshima and Nagasaki, they started the Iroquois Confederacy (the 'United Nations') only for show, and since then have established an Empire with a military presence in 153 countries, and have intervened in the affairs of 22 countries with invasions that were not even preceded by a declaration of war.

If these are the "Sons of Liberty", then I am unimpressed. I would rather be *matriotic* than patriotic, humble rather than arrogant, a citizen of another country, rather than a US citizen without any real rights anyway, since US citizens are basically citizens of the District of Columbia, and they are in fact classified today as property or franchisee of the federal government, as an 'individual entity'.

"We the people" have become *individual entities!* Slaves too, by the way, were the property of their owners!

# Complaint

Today Long Island has two remaining Indian reservations, the Unkechaug (in the Poospatuck reservation) and the Shinnecock, both in Suffolk County. There is also another Native American group, the Montauk (Montaukett), that is seeking both state and federal recognition. These tribes, bands, or traditional organisations consider themselves entirely Native American.

However, today on Long Island there is also a confederation of Native American tribes, and this one considers itself British and Native American at the same time, the Ryamecah (or Ryamecah Confederation).

Ryamecah is the name of a new indigenous or neoindigenous confederation of tribes of Long Island, and the name of the new confederation stands for the abbreviation of the words 'Restored Yamecah'. Even Long Island itself has been restored at least for Native American cultural purposes, and the Ryamecah today call it Winnecomac, a word which means 'Fine Country'.

We the Ryamecah hold these truths to be self-evident: that all Native American men are created equal, whether they be only Native American, or of mixed background or race; that all are endowed by their Creator with certain unalienable and fundamental rights, that among these are Privacy (the right of the individual), Life (the right of the family), and Liberty (the right of a government).

We the Ryamecah denounce the City of New York, the State of New York, and the United States of having turned Long Island into a divided colony of the American Empire, and Long Island remains an unfree colony without any self-determination, despite the fact that Canada, the 'fourteenth colony of British North America', is no longer a colony! Shame on you, you unfair Patriots, for the Loyalists would have been fairer and more decent with us!

We the Ryamecah denounce the City of New York, the State of New York, and the United States of having deprived us of our *historic British citizenship*, since besides dividing the Long Island country which today we call Winnecomac, and turning its people into an *untribalised* and uprooted flock of sheeple, they have also acted together in order to rescind any of the bonds we had with fellow Commonwealth citizens around the world, some whose ancestors even came from Long Island! Shame on you, you heartless *Congress-Men*, for we still consider the *King's Men* our family! You may move out of Mother Britannia's house if you wish, but you cannot lawfully deprive us of a continued relationship with our Mother, who is a virtuous lady, quite unlike that sinful French woman called 'Lady Liberty' off Winnecomac's shore, and you cannot lawfully deprive us of a continued relationship with our brothers and sisters around the Commonwealth!

We the Ryamecah denounce the City of New York, the State of New York, and the United States of the heinous crime of *taxation without representation*, since all of these entities tax us, and none of these tyrants represent us before the Commonwealth of Nations. We demand representation now, without ifs, ands, or buts, or we demand to be granted enough sovereignty to *represent ourselves*, as well as tax-free status, and total independence on our private properties! In exercising their right to self-determination, indigenous peoples have the right to autonomy or self-government in matters relating to their internal affairs, as well as ways and means for financing their autonomous functions, according to the United Nations Declaration on the Rights of Indigenous Peoples!

The City of New York, the State of New York, and the United States do not have the right to use their respective citizens as collateral against the unpayable federal, state, or city debt, in order to finance their extravagant and dissolute lifestyles, and their continued global wars favouring corporate interests. Human beings are not potential subjects of states, or slaves of states or corporations, but potential children of God, as man is not even a creature of the natural world strictly speaking, but supernatural!

We the Ryamecah do have, however, the right to be freed from the bondage of those who rule over us, but who are not superior to us in any way except in their arrogance. It shall be noted here, once and for all time, that the meek shall inherit the earth, not the arrogant, and this clearly means that the arrogant own nothing, nothing at all, and on Judgement Day (or *Yom HaDin* in Hebrew, *Yawm Ad-Din* in Arabic) they will be given the inheritance which truly belongs to them, but the earth shall not be part of that inheritance! They will have a hard time proving that they are even human beings, because human beings are divine, but that is not the way they have treated them!

We the Ryamecah, for the purpose of ending our status as complete hostages to the tyranny of the American Empire, mutually pledge to each other our Lives, our Fortunes, and our sacred Honour. So help us God!

# Long Island tribes

It is often cited in school textbooks that when Henry Hudson discovered Long Island in 1609, there were thirteen different tribes or groups of Indians living there.

There are many issues with the apparently established fact of the thirteen different Long Island tribes, but at least two major issues exist.

The first issue is that there are many variant spellings for these so-called tribes, and even a great deal of confusion among different writers.

For example, for many years historians thought that Patchogue was the name of an Indian tribe that inhabited the area on the south side of the Brookhaven town, but now it has been proven that Unkechaug was the name of the Indian tribe, and their headquarters was in Mastic. So the Unkechaug (Unquachog) and Patchogue (Patchoag) are actually the same tribe, or at least related tribes.

Another example of confusion, but of a different kind, is this: some historians have confused the place printed as *Matsepe* (which actually should have been printed as *Massepe*, a variant of Massapeag or Massapequa) — the place where in 1643 Captain John Underhill, accompanied by some Dutch soldiers, destroyed a fort, and killed some Indians — with Mespat (Maspeth), but this is an error. Yet even today in information sources such as the *Wikipedia*, the Massapequa (Marsapeague) and Mespat (Maspeth) tribes are commingled together, when they are, in fact, different tribes.

The second issue with the thirteen different Long Island tribes is that a *tribe*, and a *tribal area*, are two different things. Not only this is true, but it is quite possible that two different or unrelated tribes or bands of Native Americans on Long Island could have lived in the very same area in the past, perhaps even in harmony, as Long Island tribes in general were very peaceful tribes — unlike the often greedy and arrogant tribes outside Long Island.

Contemporary historian John A. Strong of Southampton College has shown evidence that the names commonly used to identify peoples or tribes on Long Island were instead European transliterations of indigenous language place names. For generations these place names were mistakenly used as exonyms for peoples, not places.

Native Americans on Long Island were connected by kinship systems, and communities were related by marriages and other family connections. The place the Indians lived in had a name, but not the people themselves, except as members of certain clans or social groups.

It was the Dutch who used European social order and stratification in order to describe Native Americans, but Native Americans themselves, in reality, did not view the land as divided and owned like the Dutch did. So for order and defined boundaries, the Dutch viewed the Indians they encountered as members of individual nations. The words *nations* and *tribes* were in fact used interchangeably in the Dutch records of the time.

To summarise: nobody is completely certain on the number of tribes or bands that lived on Long Island when Henry Hudson discovered Long Island in 1609, and very few certainties exist even concerning their names.

In the list that follows, we will stick with the most commonly used spellings of each of these thirteen so-called tribes, as there are far too many variants for the purpose of this book:

- Canarsie
- Cutchogue (Corchaug)
- Manhasset
- Massapequa (Marsapeague)
- Matinecock (Mantinacock)
- Merrick (Mericoke)
- Montauk (Montaukett)
- Nesaquake (Nissequaq)
- Rockaway
- Secatogue (Secatoag)

- Setauket (Setalcott)
- Shinnecock
- Unkechaug (Unquachog, Patchogue, Patchoag)

# The Ryamecah

Native Americans called the Lenape were the first people to live in what is now Queens County, New York. Research shows that the land was divided between four family groups: the Yamecah (Jameco), the Rockaway, the Mespat (Maspeth), and the Matinecock (Mantinacock).

The Lenape lived off the land in round huts made of bark and wood called wigwams. They hunted animals, gathered nuts and berries, and grew vegetables like corn, beans and squash — a dietary staple known as 'The Three Sisters' by many Eastern Woodland tribes. They also caught fish and harvested clams and oysters alongside rivers, ponds and the ocean.

Jamaica Avenue in Queens County, New York was an ancient trail for tribes from as far away as the Ohio River and the Great Lakes, who came to trade skins and furs for *wampum*, the traditional sacred shell beads of the indigenous people of North America. Wampum were used in woven belts made to commemorate treaties or historical events; for exchange in personal social transactions, such as marriages; and were often used by European colonists as currency for trading with Native Americans.

It was in 1655 that the first settlers paid the Native Americans with two guns, a coat, and some powder and lead for the land lying between the old trail and 'Beaver Pond', which later was renamed Baisley Pond.

Dutch Director-General Peter Stuyvesant dubbed the area *Rustdorp* (rest town) in granting the 1656 land patent.

The English took over in 1664, renamed the place Jameco or Yamecah; gave the same name to the Native Americans that lived in the area; and made the area a part of the county of Yorkshire. In 1683, when the British divided the Province of New York into counties, Jamaica became the county seat of Queens County, one of the original counties of New York.

The Hon. Most Rev. Dr. Cesidio Tallini, Governor of the United Micronations Multi-Oceanic Archipelago (UMMOA), Entrepreneur and Bishop, was born in the same area renamed Jameco or Yamecah by the British, and the name 'Jamaica' actually derives straight from the name of the Yamecah (Jameco) tribe or band, which means 'beaver' in the Lenape (Delaware) language they spoke — probably a Munsee language dialect.

The word Ryamecah — whose abbreviated symbols are alternatively RYMCH in Roman characters, or רימקה P, which is an interesting mix of Greek (P) and Hebrew characters (ימקה), written in Hebrew right-to-left fashion — is derived from the word Yamecah.

Ryamecah is the name of a new indigenous or neoindigenous confederation of tribes of North America, and stands for the abbreviation of the words 'Restored Yamecah'.

**Ryamecah in Greek and Hebrew characters**

The Ryamecah Confederation is a restoration of the pre-colonial and sedentary indigenous people called the Yamecah, as well as their updated sacred indigenous ways. It was started by the Hon. Tallini in order to *tribalise* or *downroot* the mainly Western, civilised, or uprooted culture of the United States.

**Ryamecah logo**

# Final complaint

The Ryamecah Confederation and its Sachem (Paramount Chief) and Medicine Man are based on the island called by Native Americans in various ways:

1. *Paumanok* ('land of tribute');
2. *Sewanhacky* ('land of sewant' or 'place of shells');
3. *Wamponomon* (often confused with wampum, but it actually means 'the east', and referred specifically to the extreme eastern point of Long Island or Montauk Point);
4. *Matouwacks* ('land of the periwinkle').

The Island's new name and its meaning

So once upon a time, the ancestors of Long Islanders called the island where they lived *Sewanhacky* or 'Sewan Country', but the members of the Ryamecah Confederation now call it Winnecomac, which means 'Fine Country'.

Certain areas of Winnecomac have also been renamed, since it doesn't make sense to use the names of the conquerors, those who still treat us and our neighbours like a colony. Ryamecah is, first and foremost, a serious attempt to recreate a modern, yet genuinely indigenous culture. Thus a clean slate is needed in order to start the new way of viewing the world.

This clean slate is needed for at least two reasons.

The first reason is ontological. One of the most cited descriptions of the concept of *indigenous* was given by José R. Martínez Cobo, a United Nations Special Rapporteur. In the famous *Study on the Problem of Discrimination against Indigenous Populations*, his working definition reads as follows:

> *Indigenous communities, peoples and nations are those which, having a historical continuity with pre-invasion and pre-colonial societies that developed on their territories, consider themselves distinct from other sectors of the societies now prevailing on those territories, or parts of them. They form at present non-dominant sectors of society and are determined to preserve, develop and transmit to future generations their ancestral territories, and their ethnic identity, as the basis of their continued existence as peoples, in accordance with their own cultural patterns, social institutions and legal system.*

It is clear from the passage cited above that neoindigenous people need some separation from their imperial and colonising foes (the City of New York, the State of New York, and the United States), in order to ensure their continued existence as distinct peoples, and for this reason the Ryamecah form at present non-dominant sectors of the colonising American society and culture.

These governments, these colonising foes, not only have turned Winnecomac into a divided colony of the American Empire, and it was not divided under Mother Britannia's gentle guardianship, but they have also deprived us of our *historic British citizenship*, in effect depriving us not only of our indigenous Native American culture, with ties to a remote Native American past, but also of our

24

special bond with the Commonwealth of Nations, with ties to a more recent European (and global) past.

The second reason a clean slate is needed is that indigenous culture is significantly different from non-indigenous culture, and this is true particularly with concern to religious views.

In the indigenous worldview the collective nature is more important than the individualistic nature emphasised in the Western worldview. To indigenous people, collective rights are more important than the narrow rights of single individuals. Also, indigenous concepts are not confined to human beings, but generally include all living things (a more holistic, but also more pagan worldview), and this emphasises the relationship of indigenous peoples to nature.

The problem with both Judaism and Christianity from a religious perspective is that they are both supernaturalistic, and there is rational reason for this because man is actually not a natural creature strictly speaking. So in both Judaism and Christianity the religious naturalistic dimension is missing entirely, and must be restored, or grafted into religious beliefs, so we can find a more accurate and sustainable balance. There is growing scientific evidence that the indigenous worldview is the more accurate one even in relation to human beings.

Our most advanced understanding of biology is beginning to indicate that even in our relationship to ourselves, there is a lot more than the simple Cartesian mind-body dichotomy would suggest, that the pluralistic, not dualistic view, is the more correct one. Ninety percent of the cells residing in the human body are actually not human cells; they are microbes.

It is often said by enlightened Christians that Christianity is not just a religion; it is a relationship with God. A more indigenous approach to religion would suggest that there is a desperate need today to widen that relationship also to the natural world that surrounds us, and that is quite significantly actually within us.

The Ryamecah are Native American and indigenous people for two reasons, not one. They have been turned into aliens with respect to other Native American tribes, both in Winnecomac (Long Island), and abroad among other Native American tribes; and they have been turned into aliens with respect to other citizens of the Commonwealth of Nations, for the United States did not just move out of Mother Britannia's house with the American Revolutionary War (1775–1783), but they also effectively caused a divorce in any relationship they had with Mother Britannia and their Commonwealth siblings!

It should be noted that with respect to the Sachem of the Ryamecah, this is entirely unfair. He is a Native American by adoption into the Nemenhah Indigenous Traditional Organization (which is acknowledged by some recognised Native American tribes, bands, or traditional communities), and he is also an Honorary Citizen of Canada.

Today the Ryamecah struggle against discrimination from Native Americans, who shamelessly allow the US government to basically dictate who is, and who is not Native American. In reality, an indigenous person is one who belongs to indigenous populations through self-identification as indigenous (group consciousness), and yet the Ryamecah are not recognised and accepted by Native Americans as one of their members (acceptance by the group) because of US government illegal interference, and this is illegal because it is a violation of their own First Amendment to the United States Constitution.

Moreover, the Ryamecah also struggle against discrimination from the Commonwealth of Nations, since they also allow the US government to basically dictate who is, and who is not a Commonwealth citizen, although by more indirect means.

Today a Commonwealth citizen, if he is not a citizen of the United Kingdom and Colonies to begin with, must be at least a citizen of any other Commonwealth country.

However, the US government basically dictates which is, and which is not a Commonwealth country, by keeping not just the United States out of the Commonwealth, and they have the authority and right to do that under International law, but also any resident of Winnecomac, including members of the Ryamecah, which they do not have the authority and right to do under International law.

The Ryamecah Sachem and Medicine Man, originally a citizen of New York State, has renounced his New York City residency as a child — these are facts anyone can check in the United States.

However, he has also renounced his New York City citizenship or potential citizenship publicly as an adult — these are facts anyone can check even outside the United States, by googling and reading an article about "Cesidio Tallini" in the *New York Times*, in which the Ryamecah Sachem and Medicine Man is basically made fun of because he firmly believes that the Kings and Queens counties are not a legal part of New York City, not according to international legal standards anyway. Tallini believes that the Kings and Queens counties are only a part of Long Island — formerly a part of the Province of New York within the Shire of York, which in turn was part of British North America, and Long Island remained British until the end of the American Revolutionary War (1775–1783), when it was left by the British, as agreed in the Treaty of Paris (1783). Tallini in that article of the *New York Times* is also made fun of not for being gay, but for being older, and still single — ie, essentially for not being a 'well-adjusted' American.

The Ryamecah Sachem and Medicine Man is made fun of in the *New York Times* article basically for being less American than black people, since he does not have the right to become the next President of the United States, but a black man can and did become the President of the United States.

The Ryamecah Sachem and Medicine Man is made fun of for being less American than gay or lesbian people, because many of these at least wish to be married under the laws (and tyranny) of the United States, while the Ryamecah carry no such suicidal or illiberal tendencies.

It should be noted that not all gays or lesbians think this way, and Sachem Wequarran is even a member of one organisation, Unmarried Equality (formerly 'Alternatives to Marriage Project'), which advocates for equality and fairness for *all unmarried people*, including people who are single, choose not to marry, cannot marry, or live together before marriage. So there are still some decent and loveable homosexual people who don't wish to needlessly flaunt their sexuality in public, as most heterosexual people actually don't flaunt their sexuality in public either, because that is considered in America, and in many other places around the world an offence, which may be deemed at least offensive or disorderly conduct by many.

So basically the Ryamecah Sachem and Medicine Man is made fun of *for being a Ryamecah*, ie for being a discriminated and indigenous minority, which considers itself distinct from any other people in Winnecomac, and in the United States!

It is okay to be gay according to the *New York Times*, but it is not okay to be single and older, because you are a discriminated and indigenous minority! Only racial and sexual discrimination is wrong, or *politically correct discrimination*, not discrimination of minorities that don't have a President in the White House, that don't have Gay Pride parades!

All of the facts stated immediately above essentially invalidate even the State of New York citizenship, and thus the United States citizenship of the Ryamecah Sachem and Medicine Man.

Moreover, the Montevideo Convention, which the United States signed, states "Even before recognition the [S]tate [or any other subject of International law, such as the Ryamecah Sachem and Medicine Man] has the right to defend its integrity and independence, to provide for its conservation and prosperity, and consequently to organize itself as it sees fit, to legislate upon its interests, administer its services, and to define the jurisdiction and competence of its courts. The exercise of these rights has no other limitation than the exercise of the rights of other [S]tates according to international law." The Sachem of the Ryamecah has the right to organise his confederation as he feels is best, to ensure its continuity as an independent or State-like entity, and to keep its indigenous culture alive and well.

Let us make this clear once and for all time: the Ryamecah Sachem and Medicine Man, also known as 'Sachem Wequarran Archimedes', is no longer a *de facto* US citizen, and cannot really be a US citizen "freely, without any mental reservation or purpose of evasion". Despite being born in the territory of the United States, Tallini never even had the full rights of a US citizen, since he was denied the opportunity to work in the field of military intelligence as a United States Marine Corps enlisted man (he does not enjoy full US federal security clearance), and essentially for that very same reason he cannot legally become the next President or Vice President of the United States!

Yet in violation of both the First Amendment to the United States Constitution, and of the Montevideo Convention, he is not allowed to be treated like the Sovereign Ryamecah Sachem and Medicine Man that he is, the Native American that he is, and the Commonwealth citizen that he should be!

More can be said about this. The place where the Sachem and Medicine Man of the Ryamecah Confederation lives is called Cutchogue, and the word *cutchogue* actually means 'headquarters'. The Sachem and Medicine Man is also arbitrarily and politically harassed by local State of New York authorities, obviously for political reasons, and also perhaps for ethnic and/or nationalistic reasons, by non-Ryamecah of the Village of South Floral Park, which claims jurisdiction over his property, but also appears to claim the right to tell the Sachem and Medicine Man how his property should be maintained.

They also call a *de facto* and perhaps even *de jure* dwelling a 'garage', so the Sachem cannot rent it, in order to help pay the extremely high and unreasonable taxes in the area, basically causing the Sachem and his loved ones a great deal of economic hardship.

The Village of South Floral Park has also violated his privacy, the rights of his family, and caused even further economic hardship by demanding unwanted and inconvenient property improvements, and while everyone in Winnecomac — not just the Ryamecah — experiences economic recession, high unemployment, and the damage caused by Hurricane Sandy (which occurred in October 2012).

Who's property is this property, we ask the State of New York, and the United States? Is it the Sachem and Medicine Man's property, and his family and loved ones' property, or is it only the property of the State of New York, and the United States, over which the Sachem and Medicine Man only pays taxes, but over which he has even lost the Right to Privacy, and thus the right to be left in peace?

After paying on Long Island some of the highest property taxes in the United States, are we also required to pay *an additional tax*, not to keep other countries from invading the United States, but also to prevent our own local and state authorities from turning private property holders, into what apparently seems today like *renters of rental property*? Is this the reason why properties across the United States have greatly lost their values lately? Is this also the fundamental reason why businesses are moving out of New York State, and even out of the United States?

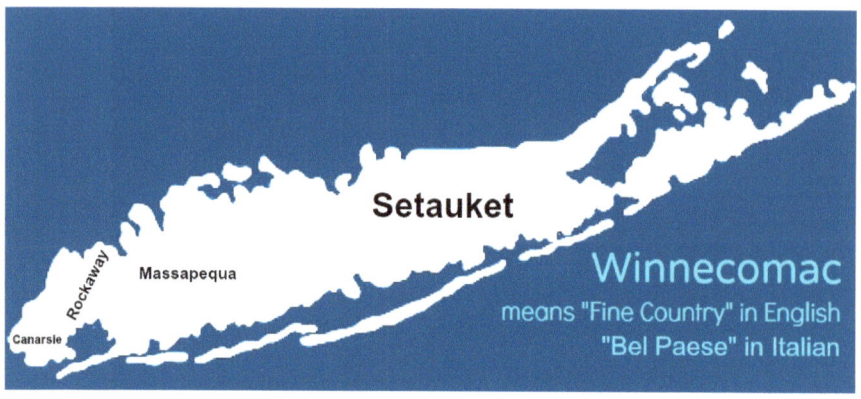

**New Island area names and Italian language details**

Another pertinent question: has the Governor of New York been harassed perhaps in his residence, or the President of the United States, by the Sachem and Medicine Man of Winnecomac (Long Island)? What is the State of New York, and the United States scared of, which they cannot apparently resolve with their criminal and politically-biased police force, and expensive armed forces if truly needed? Intelligent residents who only have the obligation to pay taxes, but no more property rights, would like to know.

It should be noted at this point that it is well-known that the Sachem and Medicine Man of Winnecomac (Long Island) does not have a police force, and he certainly has no standing or regular army. You can check that in the *Wikipedia*, by the way, since the Sachem and Medicine Man of Winnecomac is not listed in any shape or form in the *list of militaries by country*, nor is he listed in any shape or form in the *list of countries without armed forces*. So the Sachem and Medicine Man of Winnecomac (Long Island) believes that both the Governor of New York, and the President of the United States exercise illegal, disproportionate, and human rights violating power through the local village in which the Sachem and Medicine Man of Winnecomac (Long Island) lives, but does not otherwise feel a part of, since he is neither a New Yorker, nor an American!

# Civis mundi sum

The Hon. Most Rev. Dr. Cesidio Tallini is Italian, and thus European by genetics, place of citizenship, coming of age naturalisation, and primary and secondary education. Tallini was also a City of New York citizen by place of birth, but early on in life he moved outside of New York City, to a different area in New York State.

Later Tallini renounced his City of New York citizenship, or potential citizenship publicly as fully grown adult, for he firmly believes that the Kings and Queens counties are not a legal part of New York City, and only a part of Long Island. The whole island of Long Island or Winnecomac was a part of the Province of New York within the Shire of York, which in turn was part of British North America, and Long Island remained British until the end of the American Revolutionary War (1775–1783), when it was left by the British, as agreed in the Treaty of Paris (1783).

This fact essentially invalidates even his State of New York citizenship, and thus his United States citizenship. If Long Island entirely ceased to be British when the British left, and now there is no relationship between Long Island and the Commonwealth, then Tallini entirely ceased being a New Yorker when he left any City of New York allegiance, which in turn means he has also long left any State of New York allegiance, and any United States allegiance, and is in fact still being arbitrarily and politically harassed by local State of New York authorities, who have violated his civil rights, the rights of his family, and caused deliberate economic hardship.

It should also be noted that Tallini was never a full United States citizen to begin with, since he was denied the opportunity to work in the field of military intelligence as a United States Marine Corps enlisted man, and essentially for that very same reason he cannot legally become the next President of the United States.

Yet Tallini is American, as American as a Canadian (who is a Commonwealth citizen), and is American by early childhood and adult age naturalisation, and by tertiary education as well.

Tallini is also an Honorary Citizen of Canada, by the way; a Native American by adoption into the Nemenhah Indigenous Traditional Organization (which is acknowledged by some recognised Native American tribes, bands, or traditional communities); and an Ummoagian by full rights, since he is the Governor and founder of the United Micronations Multi-Oceanic Archipelago (UMMOA).

The UMMOA is a territorial nation and State, and community of nations and States, as well as a multi-oceanic archipelago accredited with, and incorporated in, the International [States] Parliament for Safety and Peace (I[S]PSP). The UMMOA is also recognised by, and affiliated with, IGOs and NGOs such as the Organization of Emerging African States (OEAS), The Multipurpose Inter-Parliamentary Union (TMIPU), and Chamber of Computer Logistics People Worldwide (which has *Special Consultative Status* with the United Nations Economic and Social Council). The UMMOA can be compared to a State, but it was created with a different mission statement, and with a different philosophical premise — the stewardship of uninhabited islands in the Pacific Ocean, Caribbean Sea, Red Sea, and Indian Ocean.

Tallini is also Native American *sui generis*, since he is the Sachem, Medicine Man, and founder of the Ryamecah, a confederation of tribes which considers itself British and Native American at the same time.

The Ryamecah Confederation shall be made up of a maximum of 14 tribes, and the names of the tribes are taken straight from the months of the Cesidian calendar, a new kind of calendar having 14 months:

1. Archimedes
2. Beethoven
3. Columbus
4. Dalí
5. Edison

6. Fleming
7. Gandhi
8. Hokusai
9. Isaiah
10. Jung
11. Kurosawa
12. Lagrange
13. Montessori
14. Nureyev

The Sachem and Medicine Man of the Ryamecah Confederation is a member of the Archimedes tribe, and has taken on the additional new name of Wequarran. Wequarran means 'Eagle'. So he is also called 'Wequarran Archimedes' in the Ryamecah Confederation, or simply 'Sachem Wequarran'.

**Ryamecah medicine wheel**

The Ryamecah Confederation is beginning to develop its own Native American culture, and they have their own medicine wheel. It is one which could have been possibly conceived by a tribe lead by the Greek Pythagoras of Samos, or in more modern times by a tribe lead by the French René Descartes, so it is very different from most Native American medicine wheels.

The Ryamecah medicine wheel is based on the new super-holistic and superrational discipline of analytic theology. It is a discipline more advanced than any science or theology taught in American universities, and the Sachem and Medicine Man of Winnecomac (Long Island) hopes to continue to develop the field of salubriology, which is based on the Ryamecah medicine wheel, since this seems quite realistic, feasible, and actually this is also his right under Article 24 of the United Nations Declaration on the Rights of Indigenous Peoples, which states, "Indigenous peoples have the right to their traditional medicines and to maintain their health practices, including the conservation of their vital medicinal plants, animals and minerals. Indigenous individuals also have the right to access, without any discrimination, to all social and health services."

The Ryamecah Confederation will continue to develop its traditional, non-alien, non-chemical patent based medicine, as is their right, and without expectation of interference from the alien and lawless FDA, or any other alien US government agency.

Giuseppe Mazzini, Italian politician, journalist and unification of Italy activist once stated: "A Country is not a mere territory; the particular territory is only its foundation. The Country is the idea which rises upon that foundation; it is the sentiment of love, the sense of fellowship which binds together all the sons of that territory." Let us therefore extend the subject of citizenship as it applies to the Sachem of the Ryamecah, who is also the Governor of the United Micronations Multi-Oceanic Archipelago (UMMOA).

Citizens of the UMMOA are *micronationalists*. Since being born in a micronation, and/or to one or more micronationalist parents, is like being physically born in Antarctica (it is like being born on an airplane unregistered in any country, or an airplane registered in Antarctica), ie all Roman law *jus soli* and *jus sanguinis* rights are effectively suspended; since everyone has the right to recognition everywhere as a person before the law (according to the Universal Declaration of Human Rights), every nationalist member of a sovereign State, and even every micronationalist is entitled to identify with a certain territory; since no distinction can legitimately be made on the basis of the political, jurisdictional, or international status of the country or territory to which a person belongs (according to the Universal Declaration of Human Rights); since international waters and the international seabed are treated legally as the common heritage of mankind (*terra communis*), and Antarctica — the only significant portion of the earth that is neither the common heritage of mankind, nor the allodial title claim of a particular sovereign State, making it at least the perfect land tenure claim over which even a micronation can exercise self-determination and independence unimpeded — is treated as no man's land (*terra nullius*); since if there is anyone on earth who can claim Antarctica as their place of citizenship it is the micronationalist, because the micronationalist is the only kind of nationalist so powerless that he is not inherently capable of endangering the pristine Antarctic environment; then Tallini, a micronationalist with a solid, and relatively long micronational history, can claim a place of citizenship in Antarctica by naturalisation!

Tallini, by the way, is also factually the Ambassador at Large of Antarctica and Unrepresented or Underrepresented Polities for The Multipurpose Inter-Parliamentary Union (TMIPU).

Tallini has also worked for the ChaRosa Foundation Corporation in the African-American community, and for the African-American community of Cambria Heights, New York for at least six years, and is today the Interim Deputy Minister of Information for the Republic of Cabinda (Kabinda); he is a qualified Attorney-at-Law for the Law Society of Cabinda; he is the Communications Director of the Organization of Emerging African States; he is the International President of the International Network of Bishops and Archbishops (founded by an African bishop); and he is also the Director for North America and Europe of The African Project.

So Tallini can claim a place of citizenship in Africa by naturalisation! It should be noted that in 1963 the Organization for African Unity recognised the division of Angola and Cabinda by ranking Cabinda the 39th State still to be decolonised, and Angola as the 35th.

More can be added. During the 7th meeting of the Committee on NGOs, held at the United Nations Headquarters in New York, the Chamber of Computer Logistics People Worldwide (CCLP Worldwide), an India-based and international NGO, was recommended for

*Special Consultative Status*, and later was granted this status with the United Nations Economic and Social Council (ECOSOC). This development became possible after Tallini managed to overcome to the persistent objections of the Distinguished Representative of Pakistan in February 2012.

Tallini today is an Additional Representative for Chamber of Computer Logistics People Worldwide at the United Nations Headquarters, an *International Life Member* of the International Council of CCLP Worldwide, and has even been called by his colleagues in India "Shri Cesidio Tallini" (Mr. Cesidio Tallini). So Tallini can also claim a place of citizenship in Asia by naturalisation!

To summarise, the Hon. Most Rev. Dr. Cesidio Tallini, also known as 'Sachem Wequarran Archimedes', is a Native American by place of birth, by adoption by a Native American indigenous and traditional organisation, and *sui generis*; he is a European by place of citizenship at birth; he is an Ummoagian, Antarctican, African, and Asian by place of citizenship by naturalisation; hopes for the Ryamecah Confederation to become a Commonwealth of Nations Member, and for all its citizens to become Commonwealth citizens; and hopes to have proven that he is a *de facto*, if not *de jure* citizen of the world, and certainly he is a subject of International law.

The HMRD Cesidio Tallini is a citizen of the world, as he has few connections only to the continent of Australia, or the region of Oceania. He hopes to become at least a little Australian when his Native American tribe is recognised as a sovereign State, and when his dream of becoming a citizen of the Commonwealth is realised. Then he will be able to join hands with Australian citizens who are Commonwealth citizens like himself, and with Indigenous Australians as indigenous as himself!

Marcus Tullius Cicero, Roman philosopher, statesman, and lawyer once stated: «*Civis mundi sum; nihil est alienum mihi.*» Translation: "I am a citizen of the world; nothing is foreign to me." Perhaps one day the HMRD Cesidio Tallini will be able to say that same Latin phrase publicly, as well as any Independent Catholic Bishop like himself can utter it, and not as a mere sentiment, but as a legal fact!

Yes, the Sachem and Medicine Man of the Ryamecah is also a Nondenominational Bishop, and an Independent Catholic Bishop, and thus has inherited a Melchizedek-Christ-Pahana triple religious progeny, and a therapeutic-religious tradition.

The politicians of the world often think solely in terms of power and strength. These worldly men and women believe that riches and glory are theirs when they assert themselves, even brutally, and take whatever they believe they are entitled to, regardless of the burden on the equal rights of others.

My question to all these leaders is this: if you are destined to inherit the earth, then why do you act like you have already been disinherited? Why do you already act like that Special Judge of Judgement Day — who is called Messiah (or *Moshiach*), Christ, *Imam Mahdi* (or 'son of Mary'), Maitreya Buddha, *Kalki Avatara*, Saoshyant, Manifestation of God, *Zhenren* (or 'True Man'), or *Pahana* in various religious traditions — has thrown the *Liber statutorum et legum Dei*, the 'Book of The Statutes and The Laws of God' at you?

The truth is this: unless we understand how destructive we are if we don't learn to respect the rights of all human beings, of all races, of all social circumstances, not just the politically correct monogamously married, and monogamously gay states; unless we understand how destructive we are if we fail to honour all the other natural creatures with which we share the earth around us, and which even inhabit the intestines within us; we are and remain weak, powerless, and spiritually bankrupt. We may believe in God, but we remain vile beings, entirely apart from the majesty of the Creator.

Blessed are the meek who shall read this book, for they shall truly inherit the earth, as was prophesied (Matthew 5:5).

# About the author

S achem Wequarran Archimedes is a Native American by place of birth; by adoption by a Native American indigenous and traditional organisation; and *sui generis*.

A Sachem is the chief of a confederation of North American Indians, and Sachem Wequarran is the paramount chief of the Ryamecah Confederation. The name Wequarran means 'Eagle', while Archimedes is the name of one of the 14 tribes that form the Ryamecah.

Sachem Wequarran is also a European by place of citizenship at birth; an Ummoagian, Antarctican, African, and Asian by place of citizenship by naturalisation; a *de facto* if not *de jure* citizen of the world; and certainly a subject of International law.

Outside of the Ryamecah Confederation Sachem Wequarran is better known as the Hon. Most Rev. Dr. Cesidio Tallini, and is the Governor of the United Micronations Multi-Oceanic Archipelago (UMMOA). The UMMOA is a territorial nation and State, and community of nations and States, as well as a multi-oceanic archipelago accredited with, and incorporated in, the International [States] Parliament for Safety and Peace (I[S]PSP).

The I[S]PSP is an intergovernmental organisation (IGO) of States whose Constitution was served to the Secretary General of the United Nations on 28 September 1976, with the acknowledgement of the Officer of the Secretary General of the United Nations; which was recognised by the United Nations as a sovereign, intergovernmental and diplomatic organ on 25 May 1979; which is incorporated in the United States, and is also a registered juridical person in Palermo, Italy; which was started with the signature of the Constitution by the Heads of State of Cyprus, Mali, Somalia, Senegal, and others; which was legally empowered in *de facto* fashion by the Treaty of Friendship between the USA and Italy (26 July 1949); and which now has diplomatic delegations and/or parliamentarians in over 180 nations. The I[S]PSP is an intergovernmental organisation (IGO) of States which is controversial among certifiable fools, since it doesn't really place the States of the world at the centre of the universe, but Man himself, as a potential subject of International law legally, and child of God theologically.

The UMMOA is also recognised by, and affiliated with, IGOs and NGOs such as the Organization of Emerging African States (OEAS), The Multipurpose Inter-Parliamentary Union (TMIPU), and Chamber of Computer Logistics People Worldwide (which has *Special Consultative Status* with the United Nations Economic and Social Council). The UMMOA can be compared to a State, but it was created with a different mission statement, and with a different philosophical premise — the stewardship of uninhabited islands in the Pacific Ocean, Caribbean Sea, Red Sea, and Indian Ocean.

Sachem Wequarran is also the President and founder of the Cesidian Root, a global Internet with over 40 root servers distributed on all major land masses except Greenland and Antarctica. He is also the Bishop and founder of the Cesidian Church; the International President of the International Network of Bishops and Archbishops; a Voting Member of the Electoral College of Bishops of the Universal Life Church World Headquarters; and a Native American Medicine Man.

Sachem Wequarran is also Deputy, Ambassador at Large, International Ambassador, or Special Representative for several IGOs and NGOs, and was even made Ambassador at Large of Antarctica and Unrepresented or Underrepresented Polities by The Multipurpose Inter-Parliamentary Union (TMIPU).

Sachem Wequarran has earned both American and Italian high school diplomas in the past; has earned several different post-secondary education diplomas and certificates, including a National Work Readiness Credential from the National Work Readiness Council, and a Certificate of Qualification to Practice from the Law Society of Cabinda; and has earned a BS degree from the University of Phoenix, another BSc degree, two religious doctorate degrees, and was awarded two honorary doctorates.

Sachem Wequarran is also the *de facto* or *de jure* author of several books in English and Italian; the father of Cesidian law, analytic theology, Cesidian salubriology, and Fourth-Fifth World studies; the developer of several indigenous and novel time, linguistic, educational, and intellectual property systems; and an independent scholar.